It Rains

KINGFISHER

NEW YORK

KINGFISHER
LONDON & NEW YORK

Copyright © Kingfisher 2012
Published in the United States by Kingfisher,
175 Fifth Ave., New York, NY 10010
Kingfisher is an imprint of Macmillan Children's Books, London.

Written and designed by Dynamo Ltd.

Distributed in the U.S. and Canada by Macmillan,
175 Fifth Ave., New York, NY 10010

Library of Congress Cataloging-in-Publication data has been applied for.

ISBN 978-0-7534-7006-0

Kingfisher books are available for special promotions and premiums. For details contact:
Special Markets Department, Macmillan, 175 Fifth Ave., New York, NY 10010.

For more information, please visit www.kingfisherbooks.com

Printed in China
9 8 7 6 5 4 3 2 1
1TR/0612/HH/-/140MA

Contents

Why does it rain?

Rain comes from clouds, which are made up of billions of water droplets. The droplets are so tiny and light that they float in the air.

Sometimes the droplets in a cloud start to join together. They get bigger and heavier until they are too heavy to float. Then they fall as rain.

All about rain

- On Mount Wai'ale'ale in Hawaii, it rains for about 350 days a year.
- In some parts of the world, it hardly ever rains.
- Rain clouds look darker than ordinary clouds because they are full of big water drops, making them thicker.

Some warm
parts of the
world get rain
almost every day

Rain helps
plants to grow

5

Why don't all clouds look the same?

The water droplets in clouds never stay still. They float around and can be blown by the wind, changing the shape of the cloud.

You can sometimes tell what the weather is going to be like by looking at cloud shapes. A cloud might get bigger and thicker as the water droplets inside it turn into raindrops.

All about clouds

- Tall storm clouds are called cumulonimbus (kew-mew-low-nim-bus) clouds.

- Big, thick rain clouds are called nimbostratus (nim-bow-strat-us) clouds.

- Puffy white clouds are called cumulus (kew-mew-lus) clouds. They look like fluffy cotton balls.

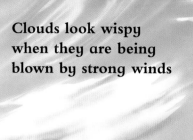

Clouds look wispy
when they are being
blown by strong winds

Low, puffy clouds
can mean rain is
on its way

A giant cloud stretching
high up into the air
means that a storm
could be coming

What is snow made of?

When the weather gets very cold, the water droplets in a cloud freeze into tiny pieces of ice called crystals.

They are too heavy to stay floating in the sky, so they fall to the ground as snow.

All about snow

- It snows most often in the far north and far south of the world and on high mountains.
- It snows most in the winter, when the weather is coldest.
- The biggest snowman ever built was 122 feet (37m) high and was actually a snowwoman.

You can build with snow
because its icy crystals
stick together well

Why is thunder so loud?

Thunderstorms happen when strong winds hurl water droplets around inside a cloud. This makes electricity that flashes down to the ground as lightning.

Lightning is super hot, and it heats up the air in its path very quickly. The heating of the air makes the loud booming noise that we call thunder.

All about thunder

- Sound takes longer to travel through the air than light, so we hear the noise of the lightning (the thunder) a few seconds after we see it.

- A bolt (streak) of lightning is very long, but only about half an inch (1cm) wide.

- There are around 2,000 thunderstorms going on in the world at any one time.

Lightning can
travel as far as
87,000 miles
(140,000km)
in one
second

You can see
lightning best when
it is dark outside

11

Why does the wind blow?

Wind is moving air. When air warms up, it gets lighter and rises up into the sky.

Colder air rushes in to fill the space left by the rising warm air. That is when you can feel the wind blowing.

All about the wind

- A hurricane is a very strong wind storm.
- Hurricane winds can blow at speeds of up to 150 miles (240km) an hour.
- The higher you go, the more powerful winds can be. At the top of a mountain or a high tower they can be very strong.

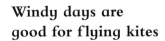

Windy days are
good for flying kites

Kites are shaped so
that the wind pushes
against them and keeps
them up in the sky

13

How big can a tornado grow?

A tornado is a spinning, twisting tube of wind that stretches down from a storm cloud and speeds across the ground.

Most tornadoes are around 150 feet (45 meters) wide, although they can sometimes be much bigger. They usually travel for a few miles and then disappear.

All about tornadoes

- The wind whirls around very fast inside a tornado.
- A tornado sucks up dust and debris as it travels along.
- The widest tornado ever measured stretched more than 2.5 miles (4km) wide.

Tornadoes appear
mainly in parts of
North America

They can do a
lot of damage,
even lifting trees
and buildings
into the air

15

Where does it hardly ever rain?

It hardly ever rains in deserts, which are the driest parts of the world. In the daytime, it can be very hot in a desert. At night, it cools down.

The biggest hot desert in the world is the Sahara Desert in North Africa. It is dry and windy there.

Deserts

- The world's driest desert is the Atacama Desert in Chile, South America.

- The Atacama can go without rain for hundreds of years.

- When places run short of water, we say they have a drought.

The Sahara is
a sandy desert

Some deserts are
rocky, not sandy

Where is it always cold?

The North and South poles are at the far north and far south of the world. The weather is always very cold there.

It is so cold in the far north and far south that the oceans freeze and become ice.

Cold places

- The coldest temperature ever measured on Earth was –128°F (–89°C)—much colder than a freezer.
- The coldest place on Earth is Vostok in Antarctica.
- Nobody lives in Antarctica all the time, but people visit bases there to do scientific experiments.

Emperor penguins
live in the far south
of the world, called
the Antarctic region

They are the tallest,
heaviest penguins
in the world

19

Why is it warm when the Sun shines?

The Sun is a giant ball of flaming gas that gives out a lot of heat. Earth travels around the Sun, so we feel its warmth.

In the summer, you will feel the Sun's rays more strongly because it is closer to you. In the winter, the Sun is farther away, so the rays are not as strong.

All about sunshine

- The summer sun can be very hot. It will damage your skin unless you cover up or wear sunscreen.

- In the summer, the Sun is so bright that people often wear sunglasses.

- Plants need the Sun to help them grow. They grow most when the weather is warm.

People go to the beach
in the summer, when
the weather is warmest

What do you know about the weather?

You can find the answers to all of these questions in this book.

Are rain clouds darker or lighter than ordinary clouds?

Do clouds stay still or move around?

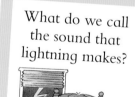

What do we call the sound that lightning makes?

What does a
tornado look like?

Is the far north of
the world a cold
place or a
warm
place?

What do we call
the driest places
in the world?

Where do you
think the coldest
place in the
world is?

23

Some weather words

Cumulonimbus A big storm cloud rising up into the sky.

Desert A very dry part of the world where rain hardly ever falls.

Drought A shortage of water when there has been too little rain.

Hurricane A huge storm with very strong winds.

Lightning A giant spark of electricity that flashes down to the ground from a storm cloud.

Thunder The noise of air being suddenly heated up by flashing lightning.

Tornado A whirling tube of wind that spins downward from a storm cloud to the ground.